Supporting Dyslexic Learners in the Secondary Curriculum

Moira Thomson, MBE

DYSLEXIA:

UNDERPINNING SKILLS FOR THE SECONDARY CURRICULUM

First published in Great Britain by Dyslexia Scotland in 2007

Second edition for schools in England published in 2017 by CPD Bytes Ltd

ISBN 978-1-912146-26-0

This booklet is 1.2 in the series

Supporting Learners with Dyslexia in the Secondary Curriculum (England)

Supporting Dyslexic Learners in the Secondary Curriculum Moira Thomson, MBE

Complete set comprises 25 booklets

1.0   Dyslexia: Secondary Teachers' Guides

1.1   Identification and Assessment of Dyslexia at Secondary School
1.2   Dyslexia: Underpinning Skills for the Secondary Curriculum
1.3   Dyslexia: Reasonable Adjustments to Classroom Management
1.4   Dyslexia: Role of the Secondary School SENCo (Dyslexia Specialist Teacher)
1.5   Partnerships with Parents of Secondary School Students with Dyslexia
1.6   Dyslexia: ICT Support in the Secondary Curriculum
1.7   Dyslexia and Examinations (Reasonable Adjustments & Access Arrangements)
1.8   Dyslexia: Information for Guidance, Pastoral & Behaviour Support Teachers) (2013)
1.9   Dyslexia: Learning Styles and Study Skills for the Secondary Curriculum NEW
1.10   Dyslexia: Role of the Teaching Assistant NEW
1.11   Dyslexia: Co-occurring & Overlapping Issues (Specific Learning Difficulties) NEW

2.0   Dyslexia: Subject Teachers' Guides
2.1   Dyslexia: Art & Design Subjects
2.2   Dyslexia: Drama (Performing Arts; Theatre Studies)
2.3   Dyslexia: English (Communication)
2.4   Dyslexia: Home Economics (Child Development; Food & Nutrition)
2.5   Dyslexia: ICT Subjects (Business Subjects; Computer Science)
2.6   Dyslexia: Mathematics (Statistics)
2.7   Dyslexia: Modern Foreign Languages
2.8   Dyslexia: Music
2.9   Dyslexia: Physical Education (Sports; Games; Dance)
2.10   Dyslexia: Science subjects (Biology; Chemistry; General Science; Physics)
2.11   Dyslexia: Social subjects (Economics; Geography; History; Citizenship Studies;
        Philosophy; Religious Studies)
2.12   Dyslexia: The Classics (Classical Greek; Latin; Classical Civilisations) (2013)
2.13   Dyslexia: Media Studies NEW
2.14   Dyslexia: Social Sciences (Anthropology; Archaeology; Humanities; Psychology;
        Sociology) NEW

Foreword by Dr Gavin Reid, formerly senior lecturer in the Department of Educational Studies, Moray House School of Education, University of Edinburgh. An experienced teacher, educational psychologist, university lecturer, researcher and author, he has made over 1000 conference and seminar presentations in more than 40 countries and has authored, co-authored and edited many books for teachers and parents.

ACKNOWLEDGEMENTS

Moira Thomson would like to thank the following for making possible the original publication of this important series of booklets:

- ✦ Dyslexia Scotland for supporting the publication and distribution of the original editions of these booklets

- ✦ The Royal Bank of Scotland for an education grant that funded Dyslexia Scotland's support

- ✦ Dr Gavin Reid for his encouragement over the years – and for writing the Foreword to these booklets

- ✦ Dr Jennie Guise of DysGuise Ltd for her support and professional advice

- ✦ The committee of Dyslexia Scotland South East for their support

- ✦ Alasdair Andrew for all his hard work and unfailing confidence

- ✦ Colleagues Maggie MacLardie and Janet Hodgson for helpful comments

- ✦ Cameron Halfpenny for proof reading and editing these booklets

- ✦ Current and former students, whose achievements make it all worthwhile

Moira Thomson MBE

2017

FOREWORD by Dr Gavin Reid

The Dyslexia booklets written by Moira Thomson have been widely circulated and highly appreciated by teachers throughout Scotland and beyond. I know they have also been used by teachers in a number of countries and this is testimony to the skills of Moira in putting together these booklets in the different subject areas of the secondary school curriculum.

It is therefore an additional privilege for me to be approached again by Moira to update this Foreword to the compendium of books developed by Moira in association with Dyslexia Scotland.

These updated guides are for all teachers - they contain information that will be directly relevant and directly impact on the practice of every teacher in every secondary school in the country. It is heartening to note that the guides again provide a very positive message to readers. The term Dyslexia is not exclusive to the challenges experienced by learners with dyslexia, but there is now a major thrust towards focussing on the strengths and particularly what they **can** do - and not what they 'can't do'. It is important to obtain a learning profile which can be shared with the student.

Moira encapsulates these points in these updated booklets. The focus is on supporting learners and helping them overcome the barriers to learning. At the same time it is important that learners with dyslexia, particularly in the secondary school develop responsibility for their own learning. The acquisition of self-sufficiency in learning and self-knowledge is an important aspect of acquiring efficient learning skills for students with dyslexia. It is this that will stand them in good stead as they approach important examinations and the transition to tertiary education and the workplace. For that reason these guides are extremely important and need to be available to all teachers. Moira ought to be congratulated in endeavouring to achieve this.

The breadth of coverage in these guides is colossal. Moira Thomson has met this immense task with professionalism and clarity of expression and the comprehensiveness of the guides in covering the breadth of the curriculum is commendable.

As well as including all secondary school subjects the guides also provide information on the crucial aspects of supporting students preparing for examinations, the use of information and communication technology, information for parents, details of the assessment process and the skills that underpin learning. It is important to consider the view that learners with dyslexia are first and foremost 'learners' and therefore it is important that their learning skills are developed fully. It is too easy to place the emphasis on developing literacy skills at the expense of other important aspects of learning. The guides will reinforce this crucial point that the learning skills of all students with dyslexia can be developed to a high level.

The guides do more than provide information on dyslexia; they are a staff development resource and one that can enlighten and educate all teachers in secondary schools. I feel certain they will continue to be warmly appreciated. The guides have already been widely appreciated by teachers and school management as well as parents and other professionals, but the real winners have been and will continue to be the **students** with dyslexia. It is they who will ultimately benefit and the guides will help them fulfil their potential and make learning a positive and successful school experience.

Dr Gavin Reid
April 2016

WHAT IS DYSLEXIA?

Dyslexia is widely recognised as a specific difficulty in learning to read.

Research shows that dyslexia may affect more than the ability to read, write and spell – and there is a growing body of research on these 'co-occurring' factors.

The Rose Report[1] identifies dyslexia as *'a developmental difficulty of language learning and cognition that primarily affects the skills involved in accurate and fluent word reading and spelling, characterised by difficulties in phonological awareness, verbal memory and verbal processing speed.'*

Dyslexia is a learning difficulty that primarily affects the skills involved in accurate and fluent word reading and spelling.

Characteristic features of dyslexia are difficulties in phonological awareness, verbal memory and verbal processing speed.

Dyslexia occurs across the range of intellectual abilities.

It is best thought of as a continuum, not a distinct category, and there are no clear cut-off points.

Co-occurring difficulties may be seen in aspects of language, motor co-ordination, mental calculation, concentration and personal organisation, but these are not, <u>by themselves,</u> markers of dyslexia.

A good indication of the severity and persistence of dyslexic difficulties can be gained by examining how the individual responds or has responded to well-founded intervention.

Rose Report page 10

Dyslexia exists in all cultures and across the range of abilities and socio-economic backgrounds. It is a hereditary, life-long, neuro-developmental condition. Unidentified, dyslexia is likely to result in low self-esteem, high stress, atypical behaviour, and low achievement.[2]

Estimates of the prevalence of dyslexia vary according to the definition adopted but research suggests that dyslexia may significantly affect the literacy attainment of between 4% and 10% of children.

---

[1] Rose, J (2009) *Identifying and Teaching Children and Young People with Dyslexia and Literacy Difficulties* DCFS Publications - independent report to the Secretary of State for Children, Schools & Families June 2009 http://webarchive.nationalarchives.gov.uk/20130401151715/http://www.education.gov.uk/publications/eOrderingDownload/00659-2009DOM-EN.pdf

[2] From Scottish Government working definition of dyslexia http://www.gov.scot/Topics/Education/Schools/welfare/ASL/dyslexia

TEACHERS' RESPONSIBILITIES RE LEARNERS WITH DYSLEXIA

References: Part 6 of the Equality Act 2010; Part 3 of the Children and Families Act 2014

All children/young people are entitled to an education appropriate to their needs that promotes high standards and the fulfilment of potential - to enable them to:

- achieve their best
- become confident individuals living fulfilling lives
- make a successful transition into adulthood, whether into employment, further or higher education or training

SEND Code of Practice 0-25[3]

All schools have duties towards individual young people to identify and address any Special Educational Needs/Disability (SEND). Dyslexia that has a substantial, long-term, adverse impact on day-to-day learning may be identified as both SEN and a disability.

Teachers' responsibilities for meeting the needs of dyslexic learners are the same as those for all students, and should include approaches that avoid unnecessary dependence on written text.

Teachers have a responsibility to provide a suitably differentiated subject curriculum, accessible to all learners, that provides each with the opportunity to develop and apply individual strengths – and to ensure that learners with SEND get the support they need to access this. Rose[4] suggests that all teachers should have 'core knowledge' of dyslexia characteristics – to help them to make adjustments to their practice that will prevent discrimination and substantial disadvantage.

Dyslexia may be difficult for some teachers to identify in a subject context – some think that dyslexia has little or no impact in their subject – others believe that dyslexia will have been resolved at primary school. The impact of unsupported dyslexia on learning in secondary subject classrooms may be profound, and result in a mismatch between a student's apparent subject ability and the quality (and quantity) of written work.

While subject teachers are not expected to diagnose dyslexia without specialist input, they should be aware of its core characteristics and likely manifestations in the classroom so they may refer students to the SENCo (or specialist teacher) for assessment. Many schools have checklists and questionnaires in place to help teachers identify possible SEN and subject teachers should use these and follow established procedures when they suspect that dyslexia might be present.[5]

---

[3] SEND Code of Practice 0-25
https://www.gov.uk/government/uploads/system/uploads/attachment_data/file/398815/SEND_Code_of_Practice_January_2015.pdf
[4] Rose Report (2009) page 17
[5] A version of a Dyslexia Indicators Checklist for secondary age students is provided at the end of this booklet

SUBJECT TEACHERS' GRADUATED APPROACH TO DYSLEXIA SUPPORT SHOULD INCLUDE:

- Awareness of the learning differences related to dyslexia that may cause difficulties within the subject curriculum

- Acknowledgement of the very severe difficulties some dyslexic learners experience due to failure to master early stages of literacy and numeracy

- Understanding that dyslexia is developmental in nature and that some students who coped with the early stages of literacy acquisition may begin to experience difficulties with higher order skills and processing issues in the secondary curriculum

- Selection or design of appropriate teaching and learning programmes that match the range of all abilities, within the curricular framework of the school

- Commitment to the need to reduce barriers to learning linked to the delivery of the curriculum as well as those due to the impact of dyslexia

- Acceptance that some learners with dyslexia may require additional support within the context of a subject and to consult with parents, colleagues and specialists (and the young person) to determine how best to provide this

- Willingness to ask for advice and support from the SENCo and/or specialist teacher if a dyslexic learner does not make the expected progress towards achieving outcomes identified in the SEN Support Plan

- Understanding that, while dyslexia is not linked to ability, able dyslexic learners may persistently underachieve

- Knowledge that many dyslexic learners use strategies such as misbehaviour or illness for coping with difficulties they do not necessarily understand themselves

- Taking account of the difficulties experienced by dyslexic learners when reviewing progress so that subject knowledge and ability are assessed fairly by making reasonable adjustments to arrangements for assessments (Access Arrangements) that reflect the additional support usually provided in the classroom

Dyslexic learners constantly meet barriers to learning across the curriculum and may become discouraged very quickly due to lack of initial success in subject classes. This may result in subject teachers assuming that they are inattentive or lazy, when they are actually working much harder than their classmates, but with little apparent effect.

UNDERPINNING SKILLS FOR THE SECONDARY SCHOOL CURRICULUM

Most secondary teachers assume that students will arrive from primary school with the ability to read, write and compute at a level that allows them to access the secondary curriculum. But they are also aware of the need to make reasonable adjustments in the classroom to meet the needs of learners whose SEND may result in barriers to learning in their subject. This has led to the introduction of 'dyslexia friendly' whole school initiatives — usually described in a school's SEN support - and pro-active teaching approaches that anticipate and minimise/remove possible barriers to learning.

The graduated approach to meeting individual SEN requires subject teachers to evaluate **how** the impact of dyslexia - as described in a student's profile - may affect learning in their particular subject in order to identify strategies to meet subject-specific learning outcomes, including those identified in a student's SEN support plan.

For year 7, transition arrangements with associated primary schools will usually have provided details of individual students' known strengths and identified any reasonable adjustments or strategies that were effective in the achievement of outcomes in the SEN support plan. However, analysing these to inform a student profile for the secondary curriculum that might be used to predict activities/content that may give rise to the need for additional support for as many as 15 different subject teachers will be a daunting task for a SENCo or specialist teacher who does not yet know the new students.

Lists of underlying difficulties associated with dyslexia may not be particularly useful to help secondary subject teachers to determine what additional support may be needed in their classroom. They often find general comments about possible barriers to learning more informative – e.g. *this student experiences difficulties with processing language* - may not be particularly helpful, **but** *this student may be unable to read/write at the same rate as the rest of the class* immediately informs a teacher where adjustments/supportive interventions may be needed.

If comments of this nature also indicate previously successful strategies for minimising the impact of dyslexic issues – and identify student strengths - subject teachers are more likely to remove barriers to learning and introduce effective provision to meet the individual needs of dyslexic students in their subject.

UNDERPINNING ACADEMIC SKILLS

The academic skills required for students to access the secondary subject curriculum are:
Communication skills - reading, writing, listening/watching, talking
Study skills– involving auditory/verbal processing, visual processing and short-term (working) memory, sequencing – and subject-specific issues such as computation, note-taking and exams

Practical skills - organisation, spatial awareness, directional/positional/temporal issues, gross/fine motor skills, co-ordination, handwriting, use of tools/ equipment, playing team games etc.

Not all dyslexic students will experience difficulties in all of these areas, and many will demonstrate strengths in areas where other students may struggle. A dyslexic student's profile - and SEN support plan - should identify both known strengths and probable difficulties, according to the demands of each subject.

COMMUNICATION

LITERACY and [handwritten]

Most subject teachers expect dyslexic students to have issues with reading and spelling – but not all will experience the same difficulties – and many may already have developed coping strategies - some of which may not be effective in the secondary curriculum.

READING ISSUES

Reading in the subject curriculum has a number of different functions, most of which are likely to be impacted to some degree by dyslexia. Dyslexic students who are quick to understand and respond in class often read much more slowly than teachers would expect.

VISUAL ISSUES

Some students may experience visual stress – which may exacerbate any visual processing issues in a dyslexic profile and have a negative impact on reading, though – once identified – this may be ameliorated by putting simple adjustments in place.

When reading, students who experience visual stress may
- complain of headaches, dizziness or nausea when reading at length
- report that words move around the page or the text is too bright
- experience visual distortions or discomfort when working with dense print
- rub their eyes, blink rapidly and often when reading
- be unable to see/locate information on a whiteboard

Reasonable Adjustments to minimise visual stress issues: There are a number of options in this area including the use of tinted overlays or lenses, but these may require action by young people and their parents. **Teachers might**
- enlarge print or change font and increase line spacing in print materials
- provide text on coloured paper chosen by the student
- encourage the use of coloured overlays or reading rulers
- provide audio/electronic version of longer texts
- scan/load text into a computer to take advantage of text-speech software but remain aware that a computer screen reader may hinder rather than help with some text materials as these may not read numbers/formulae accurately
- Enlarge graphs/diagrams to make details more readily accessible
- take action to minimise glare/reflected light on the whiteboard

- find out which colours are difficult to read on the whiteboard and not use these
- set the background on an interactive board to a colour (chosen by students)
- vary classroom/studio lighting to minimise glare and visual stress
- provide alternative versions of material presented on the white/interactive board
- seat the student out of direct sunlight and away from fluorescent lighting

Note: It is important that teachers check that students' eyes have been tested by an optometrist to identify any visual impairment that can be corrected through treatment or prescription lenses.

READING FOR INFORMATION

Many dyslexic students have difficulty remembering what they have just read and they may reach the end of a page and have no idea what it is about. They often have to re-read texts, slowing their reading rate considerably and making them fall behind the rest of the class.

Barriers to reading for information: dyslexic students may
- read more slowly than classmates, so may not finish set reading tasks
- give up easily when faced with long texts and small print
- forget what they have just read and have to re-read text to make sense of content
- omit or insert words or sentences from another place on the page impacting comprehension of text
- misread words, changing the meaning of text
- lose the place often - having to start again from the top of the page
- have difficulty locating information in a text source
- have difficulty in pin-pointing the main idea in a passage
- fail to identify a diagram, table, chart or graph as an integral part of text
- struggle with the flow of reading, when it is not from left to right, as when it includes labelled tables and annotated diagrams
- be unable to use text versions of dictionaries, directories, encyclopaedias, indexes

Reasonable adjustments: teachers should try to ensure that print is not the only source of subject information for students.
- ensure that all text materials are clear and legible
- highlight key words/information in text
- use colour codes for e.g. character/place names in texts so students do not confuse these
- issue large print versions of text materials to help dyslexic students to find the place more easily
- number lines and paragraphs and give specific references of location of information
- provide opportunities for discussion of topics – paired or small groups
- use video or audio recordings to support/illustrate text content
- introduce an electronic reading pen for decoding individual words/phrases
- provide visual, audio or electronic versions of class notes and instructions

- arrange access to a scanner and a computer with text to speech software
- provide electronic dictionaries and online references

Note: Recording or scanning materials for students is often less simple than it appears – staff should be alert to copyright issues.

READING ALOUD

Even those dyslexic students who are making good progress with reading may panic if asked to read in public and progress may be jeopardised by the experience. Many of the problems experienced by dyslexic students when reading for information are present when shorter texts are concerned. For many, even the thought of reading aloud in class, in front of peers is a nightmare. However, it is possible for the teacher to arrange a signal to alert a dyslexic student when they will be called on to read, allowing some preparation time – or even arrange and rehearse a passage in advance. This includes the dyslexic student in the class activity and may lead to improved self-esteem and developing confidence.

Barriers to reading aloud: dyslexic students may
- experience visual distortions, especially when they are stressed, that make it difficult for them to focus on text to be read
- have to sound out longer, and unfamiliar words, preventing them from reading with fluency and often obscuring meaning
- reverse words or phrases, insert or omit small words, sometimes changing meaning of text
- unintentionally insert words/phrases from the line above or below
- lose the place when reading, for no apparent reason
- be very sensitive to being corrected publicly, adversely affecting self-esteem
- be embarrassed by their lack of reading fluency, resulting in distress or inappropriate behaviour

Reasonable adjustments: when reading aloud by students is an essential part of a lesson, teachers should ensure that dyslexic students are given their segment well in advance to allow them to rehearse and resolve any possible difficulties. They should
- never ask a student with dyslexia to read aloud **without advance warning**
- issue set texts well in advance so that dyslexic students can learn new vocabulary and prepare for reading aloud
- ensure that key subject information is read aloud only by a teacher or a competent reader
- provide visual support that will enable dyslexic students who have auditory-verbal difficulties to process the information being read aloud
- accept the dyslexic as a volunteer reader – sometimes students prepare a section of text and want to read it to the class, so provide the opportunity for this to happen

Note: Some dyslexic students may read aloud (privately) when reading for information – some times when walking around the room. This multi-sensory approach enables them to process a text more quickly as they are able to use strengths to support weaknesses – e.g. reading aloud brings auditory strengths to support weak visual processing.

CLOSE READING - TESTING SUBJECT KNOWLEDGE

In many subjects, understanding of a topic may be tested or reinforced by a reading passage followed by a number of questions, by multiple choice exercises or by students filling blanks in a passage using key words (Cloze). In exercises of this nature, the reading ability of a student will often determine success rather than knowledge or understanding of the facts or concepts being tested. Subject teachers should bear in mind that it takes dyslexic students longer to read the questions, compose answers in their heads, and get them down on paper, and that their entitlement to additional support extends to all assessments, even spot topic tests.

Barriers to close reading assessments: dyslexic students may
- be unable to complete close reading in the same time as peers
- struggle to locate key words in the text passage
- be unable to recognise key words out of context
- have difficulty remembering subject vocabulary
- have to re-read an entire passage from the beginning so that it makes sense
- be unable to relate the questions to the passage
- have difficulty with multiple-choice questions due to the volume of reading required to answer these correctly and the similarity of choices offered

Reasonable adjustments: teachers might
- identify a 'reading buddy' to help a dyslexic student in class reading activities
- use pair or group discussions to complete revision exercises
- create the opportunity for student/teacher discussion
- set practical tasks instead of using tests requiring fluent reading skills
- encourage students to draw up tables, or to complete charts rather than filling-in blanks
- provide alternatives to reading passages, such as using illustrations for interpretation of subject content
- conduct a class review session before the test
- provide a study guide for students giving key terms and concepts
- always provide a list of vocabulary required to complete any Cloze exercise
- encourage the use of ICT to complete Cloze exercises
- arrange extra time for dyslexic students to complete a test

Note: Dyslexic students should be given the same level of support for assessments that is normally provided in the subject classroom.

WRITING ISSUES

The written work of dyslexic students is often illegible, with bizarre spelling, little punctuation and poor organisation. While most can, with an effort, provide some written work, which is legible by teachers who know them, this may take a very long time to produce.

Dyslexic students are often acutely aware of their difficulties and are very self-conscious about written work, often feeling frustrated by their inability to express their understanding through writing. This makes it difficult for them to demonstrate their grasp of a subject to the same extent as other students. There is often a huge difference between their ability to tell you something and their ability to write it down. They tend to avoid writing whenever possible and may have developed a range of strategies to avoid writing.

WRITTEN ASSIGNMENTS

It is very difficult for dyslexic students to plan written work and follow an ordered sequence in the development of their ideas. In some subjects, like English, teachers demonstrate how to write essays of different types and give students a framework, or plan to follow. There may be an assumption in other subject areas, that students already know how to produce well-structured extended written responses, and teachers do not see it as their responsibility to teach this.

However, no matter what the experience and skills of the rest of the class, dyslexic students need subject-specific instruction in how to structure written work, as they are often unable to transfer skills acquired in one subject to a different context. Many subject teachers who undertake this teaching input have identified great improvement of the written work of all students, not just those who are dyslexic.

Barriers to writing: dyslexic students may
- avoid writing whenever possible
- be unable to write quickly and legibly and take longer than other students to complete written work
- find it difficult to plan and organise extended writing
- be unable to write in the required format
- have difficulty sequencing their written work logically
- lose the thread when they are writing resulting in messy and poorly sequenced work
- become confused - having to start again, or draw arrows and lines to show insertions
- produce a poor standard of written work compared with oral ability
- give only brief written responses that do not reflect the full extent of subject knowledge and understanding
- lack fluency when writing due to word-finding, spelling and sequencing issues
- have difficulty in selecting appropriate subject terminology

- produce scrappy, illegible written pieces full of spelling mistakes, but often to the point
- cross out/erase spellings several times, even when correct
- be unable to spell the words they want, so they use simple alternatives
- have difficulty with punctuation and grammar, often writing everything as one very long sentence
- be unable to write quickly and legibly when developing material
- struggle to copy, annotate text materials or take dictated notes
- tire more quickly than others when writing so that the quality of writing deteriorates over time
- have slow laborious handwriting and be unable to keep up with speed of thought, resulting in omissions
- when proof reading, read back what they wanted to say, not what is actually written on the page
- have difficulty identifying errors in their writing, making redrafting very difficult

Reasonable adjustments: teachers might
- provide a framework for different types of subject writing
- model/provide 'skeleton' versions of the required format of written responses
- issue writing guidelines and paragraph headings to support the structure of extended writing
- teach the use of sketches and symbols as well as words to annotate text material
- use mind mapping, bullet points and visual representation to help with planning and structure and for developing story lines in imaginative writing
- encourage students to work in note form, concentrating on key words or terms
- provide visual, audio or electronic versions of notes and instructions
- provide ICT for written work and make sure that editing features and spellchecker are used
- provide an electronic word list to help with spelling for Internet searches
- allow rests when extended writing is required
- accept alternatives to extended writing e.g. charts, diagrams, pictorial representations
- permit the use of audio/digital recorders to be saved as voice files or transcribed later
- highlight errors in writing and suggest possible corrections/amendments for redrafting
- not penalise a dyslexic student for poor presentation of work or bizarre spelling, marking only on the content of an assignment

Note: Students should be made aware that poor spelling, punctuation and grammar may result in loss of marks in some exam subjects – and that Access arrangements will not prevent this.

LISTENING/WATCHING AND OBSERVATION ISSUES

Dyslexic students often struggle to respond appropriately to questions in class due to the need to process the language first before being able to process the question and formulate an answer. Some have even undergone extensive hearing tests because of the significant delay between hearing something and responding to it – despite quick reactions to e.g. sudden noises. Some dyslexic students experience auditory processing difficulties resulting in e.g. misuse of familiar words, incorrect sentence structure and difficulty remembering new or unfamiliar words.

If a teacher speaks quickly, or gives too much information at once, dyslexic students may catch only parts of this, and may be reluctant to admit that they missed information, preferring the teacher and classmates to believe that they were not paying attention. Dyslexic students may be slow to respond to a teacher's spoken instructions and find that the rest of the class is getting on with a piece of work while they have no idea where to begin - so a dyslexic student may ask *What page are we on?* immediately after the teacher has told the class the page number.

Barriers to listening/observing: dyslexic students may
- lose track of what is spoken by whom in the classroom – so may fail to respond to questions/instructions
- be unable to concentrate on listening/watching due to visual distractions and background noise
- misunderstand complicated oral questions
- think they are listening/observing but cannot concentrate
- be unable to process teacher talk at the required speed and 'hear' only part of this

Reasonable adjustments: teachers might
- provide an attention focus for listening that is directly relevant to lesson content
- provide visual support to enable dyslexic students to process oral information – e.g. labelled pictures of artefacts
- teach subject-specific terminology as 'foreign' language vocabulary and allow extra time to process this
- use class questioning to support dyslexic students to fill any gaps
- always summarise any discourse and repeat oral contributions made by other students
- ensure that key subject information is read aloud only by a competent reader
- add visual or kinaesthetic cues to reinforce tone of voice – e.g. adding a gesture or facial expression
- create visual, audio or electronic versions of notes and activity directions so dyslexic students can focus on listening/watching in class instead of trying to take notes
- allow use of a 'fidget toy' when listening/watching to aid concentration

TALKING ISSUES

Barriers to talking: dyslexic students may
- become confused when asked to talk/make a presentation in class
- have word finding problems - be unable to name a common object
- lose track of what they are saying – often repeating themselves or 'drying up' completely
- struggle to use correct vocabulary – they may feel humiliated when they mispronounce words or use the 'wrong' word
- fail to respond to questions even when they know the answer

Reasonable adjustments: teachers might
- be aware that short-term memory problems contribute to difficulties with learning vocabulary and subject facts
- give 'thinking time' to allow dyslexic students to process input and construct an appropriate response
- ask students to repeat aloud the question you have just asked
- teach the use of prompt cards and slide presentations for sequencing and illustrating oral presentations
- encourage the use of physical prompts e.g. listing items using fingers
- set up a gesture code for dyslexic students to indicate they want to answer

DISCUSSION ISSUES

Some course requirements require the promotion of discussion within the classroom for all students. Teachers may introduce topics in formal or scientific language, but it will be understood by all students in terms of how they can relate it to their own language and past experience, a process best promoted through discussion.

Barriers to learning: in discussion, dyslexic students may
- have to process the language, then the content of others' remarks, causing them to respond after others have moved on
- be unable to hold a list of discussion questions/instructions in memory and confuse the sequence of responses required
- appear not to listen in discussion/brainstorming groups, so hesitate to participate, limiting spontaneity
- have problems with turn-taking and interrupt others to make comments
- often forget what they wanted to say when their turn comes so may contribute apparently irrelevant remarks

Reasonable adjustments for discussion: teachers might
- give a structure for discussion – even issue a 'script'
- encourage students to suggest explanations, test hypotheses, challenge each other's understanding, in turn

- be aware that short-term memory problems contribute to difficulties with turn-taking and relevance
- ensure that other students are aware that some will take much longer than others to contribute appropriately
- arrange for turn-taking signals when brainstorming to enable students with dyslexia to contribute ideas as they occur to ensure that originality and creativity is not lost

STUDY SKILLS ISSUES

The secondary curriculum offers additional challenges that put considerable pressure on dyslexic students, who have problems with phonological processing and short-term memory. Many experience short-term memory limitations, finding it hard to remember arithmetic tables, the alphabet or classroom instructions. They may have difficulty organising life around a timetable and forget which books to take to school on any given day and they often cannot remember instructions just after they were given.

PROCESSING

Students with dyslexia often lack fluency and automaticity when reading/writing – despite excellent oral skills - so they may take more time than others to think, question, deduce, and form opinions – before responding to a visual or auditory stimulus. Those who also experience specific difficulties in Maths may be further disadvantaged when calculation, measurement and direction are required in practical activities.

For example - a dyslexic student may fully understand the teacher's spoken introduction to a topic but be unable to follow written instructions for class activities.

Barriers to learning: dyslexic students may
- approach new tasks with an expectation of failure
- take longer than others to respond to direction/instructions
- be very disorganised and fear new situations
- confuse verbal instructions due to working memory issues
- appear to avoid set work (because of confusion about what is required)
- misinterpret written instructions – leading to e.g. wrongly responding to comprehension questions or carrying out the wrong task
- struggle to keep to a paragraph plan or outline either going out of sequence or adding/omitting planned elements
- be unable to make personal notes or annotate printed materials because of their difficulties finding/keeping the place
- tire more quickly than others when reading/writing so that the quality of work deteriorates over the course of a lesson
- sacrifice originality and creativity to complete an activity in the time allowed

Reasonable Adjustments: teachers might

- deliver teacher-led class lessons when possible, using a variety of teaching styles
- allow extra time for dyslexic learners to practice skills and techniques
- keep classroom activities as open-ended as possible – allow a range of styles or outcomes
- encourage students to try different approaches to/interpretations of activities
- create extra time for dyslexic students to complete reading/writing tasks
- keep classroom activities as open-ended as possible – allow a range of outcomes
- encourage students to try different types of response as alternatives to writing
- ask students to repeat instructions aloud - this not only provides a check that they have understood, but they remember things better if they hear themselves speak
- offer a 'spelling' list of commonly used subject terminology to address word finding issues and avoid confusion of similar sounding terms
- number the steps or devise flow charts for e.g. the stages in report writing – or provide a checklist to follow
- provide simple sources for classroom activities, using visual, auditory and tactile starting points
- use audio-visual sources of subject matter, e.g. TV documentaries, schools programmes, current affairs discussions etc. to help set course content in context
- ensure that a screen text reader is available when internet searches are undertaken as reading issues may prevent the selection of appropriate websites to review

SHORT TERM (WORKING) MEMORY

Barriers to Learning: dyslexic students may

- lose themselves and their possessions frequently – and are unable to retrace their steps as they have no memory of what these were
- struggle with working memory, so cannot remember their subject timetable
- have difficulty remembering to bring books/equipment/homework on the correct day
- be unable to remember instructions from one moment to the next
- may misunderstand complex sequences of instructions and struggle to carry out a sequence of actions in the right order
- be unable to retrieval phonological information from long term memory due to inadequate storage of information about words – 'forgetting' names of common objects and people
- have word-finding difficulties that cause the mind to go blank mid-sentence
- struggle to learn the alphabet, days of the week, months of the year in order
- be unable to learn multiplication tables, number bonds and other sequences
- be unable to hold numbers in their heads while doing calculations
- forget what they were going to say, while waiting for a pause in the conversation or in the middle of a sentence

Reasonable adjustments: teachers might
- write the date and any page numbers on the board, always in the same place – to provide a reminder
- read information/questions aloud in chunks to help dyslexic students process meaning and develop working memory capacity
- arrange extra time and practice for dyslexic students to reinforce memory
- give only one instruction at a time/repeat instructions in sequence often
- provide written versions or repeat oral questions so dyslexic students do not have to remember these while accessing working memory
- issue summaries of set texts to help with short term memory problems
- number the steps or devise flow charts for activities or provide checklists of items
- develop a mantra for remembering the sequence of actions in an activity – e.g. *'in, over, through and out'* – when knitting
- help learners to develop rhythm when learning e.g. literary quotes or science facts - e.g. use rap, music (e.g. substitute a quotation for the lyrics of a favourite pop song), beating time, tapping feet – even invent a dance routine
- teach mnemonics and rhymes or use 'rap' or action poems to be recited when carrying out an activity
- encourage the use of memory aids for routine activities – e.g. a rubber band on the wrist to indicate left
- use visualisation and highlighting and/or colour coding to aid recall of sequences/ develop a sequenced checklist for investigation procedures
- suggest reminders for practical activities – e.g. different coloured highlighters, sticky notes
- bear in mind that all students remember bizarre or amusing incidents more easily and incorporate these in subject delivery to teach key concepts

NOTE-TAKING

Dyslexic students may experience great difficulty taking dictated notes. For those who have an auditory-verbal processing deficit or short term memory problems, it may be impossible. Many also have great difficulty making personal notes from text, video, audio or ICT sources.

Barriers to learning: when taking notes, dyslexic students may
- be unable to keep up with the writing rate of the rest of the class
- have difficulty processing what the teacher is saying
- find it impossible to listen and write at the same time
- get stuck on how to spell a particular word and be unable to proceed
- have difficulty reading/understanding their own notes
- be unable to organise personal notes into sections that make sense for study and revision
- copy chunks of text instead of writing notes in their own words

Reasonable adjustments: teachers might

- provide printed or electronic notes in advance
- identify a partner whose notes can be photocopied
- provide copies of notes as soon as possible after a lesson
- allow the use of an audio recorder so that dictated notes are accurately taken
- when dictating, spell out any technical or difficult words for all students
- provide skeleton notes indicating where students write specified information
- provide summaries of e.g. chapters of books to support students' note-taking skills
- create a framework for note-taking to help dyslexic students organise their own notes
- teach the use of bullet points and summaries for note-taking
- allow the use of mind maps, charts and diagrams for note-taking

COPYING

For some students who have dyslexia copying may be impossible. The results will certainly be unreliable and inaccurate. When copying, a dyslexic student looks up and visually "grabs" just one or two letters at a time, perhaps repeatedly sub-vocalising the names of those letters, then stares intensely at the paper when writing those one or two letters. This process is repeated over and over, with the student concerned rarely demonstrating any comprehension of the content of the copied material.

Barriers to learning: when copying, dyslexic students may

- find looking from board to desk every few seconds slow, painful, and tedious
- have very poor handwriting so are unable to read their own writing after an interval - even a very short one
- frequently lose the place so may omit material or copy it twice
- mis-spell copied words
- do not match capitalisation or punctuation when copying

Reasonable adjustments: when asking students to copy essential course material e.g. diagrams - teachers might

- provide accurate copies of material for dyslexic students – which may be studied while others copy
- create alternative copying tasks – e.g. ask dyslexic students to annotate a diagram or fill in blanks in a copy of the material
- arrange for dyslexic students to download and save materials being copied from the school network – and print if required

Note: For younger students, the teacher should make clear arrangements for the copying rather than leave it to the discretion of the students. When older, students can be expected to take the responsibility for copying. **Unsupported copying should NEVER be the ONLY source of information.**

NUMERACY ISSUES

Memorising mathematical facts (not personally interesting or relevant) is extremely difficult for many dyslexic students who experience difficulties in retaining number facts and tables, number order and sequencing.

Barriers to learning: dyslexic students may
- copy numbers incorrectly – may reverse/invert numbers
- start calculations from the wrong place – e.g. add from left to right
- have difficulty understanding place value
- be unable to estimate
- cannot align columns of figures correctly – may include the number of the question in a calculation
- find it impossible to plot accurately or extract accurate information from graphs
- often know how to do every step in the sequence, but get the steps out of order, ending up with the wrong answer
- be unable to memorise addition and subtraction facts or multiplication tables
- be unable to complete mental computation because they cannot hold numbers in their heads (working memory) while carrying out calculations
- not show working - may "see" Maths in their head, so cannot show working

Reasonable adjustments: teachers might
- avoid introducing unnecessarily complex language into a Maths assignments
- issue squared paper to help with place value and alignment of columns
- write question numbers and marks allocated in clearly defined margins to prevent these being accidentally included in a calculation
- use a reading ruler or **L** shaped card to read information from tables of figures
- encourage students to say numbers aloud as they write to prevent errors
- enlarge graphs to make details more readily accessible
- teach how to generate addition/subtraction/multiplication grids to aid computation - make these grids and 'ready-reckoners' available in class to speed up work rate
- make use of a variety of approaches (including computer games and rap/jingles) to develop and reinforce number facts
- teach strategies for developing a systematic approach to calculations, highlighting where to start and the direction of the next step
- teach 'tables' gimmicks like finger tables, use of patterns, using colour coding, verbalising using rhythm and rhyme, even music to aid recall
- demonstrate the required format for written calculations- give a sample solution showing required layout, clearly showing location for working

SHAPE/SYMBOL CONFUSION

Some students with dyslexia have problems with the identification of shapes and symbols and in discriminating between different symbols – e.g. degrees, percentages etc. There may be particular difficulties when writing indices, as these are easily portrayed inappropriately. Many dyslexic students struggle to transfer skills/knowledge gained in one subject to another context – often resulting in increased confusion when shapes/symbols are used differently.

Barriers to learning: some dyslexic students may

- mix up the symbols **+ x % $^\circ$**
- not understand or confuse subject language referring to symbols and shapes
- have particular difficulties with formulae notation
- be unable to relate the properties of a shape to its name
- have difficulty making connections between shapes
- have no idea of proportion or scale

Reasonable adjustments: teachers might

- allow enough time for the dyslexic student to process the nature of a problem
- teach the subject words that refer to symbols and issue reference cards
- display symbols charts in the classroom so that students may check these unobtrusively
- teach notation slowly and issue formulae prompts
- issue templates or stencils to emphasise the different qualities of shapes
- use colour to code lines and symbols that identify aspects of shapes
- always use visual representations of shapes to illustrate properties and names
- provide real-life examples/illustrations to help with understanding of scale/ proportion
- issue illustrated notes showing key words, diagrams explaining shape/symbol use

PRACTICAL SKILLS

Some dyslexic students appear clumsy and uncoordinated and many also seem to lack personal organisation and spend a disproportionate amount of time looking for books and equipment. There may be a need to open a dialogue with students and parents about the stress reducing powers of e.g. Velcro and slip on shoes to avoid embarrassing moments in changing rooms or about arranging extra lessons and a lot of practice - after school or out of school – for complex physical activities and road safety.

ORGANISATIONAL ISSUES

- have difficulty organising work space – misplace books and equipment
- frequently forget essential books, equipment and homework – or may carry all books all the time
- have difficulty finding/keeping the place in a text, locating notes in a workbook or

finding files on a computer
- have difficulty following a sequence of instructions in the right order
- sacrifice originality and creativity to complete an activity in the time allowed

Reasonable adjustments: teachers might
- repeat a series of instructions one at a time and relate these to visual demonstrations of actions or equipment use where possible
- number the steps or devise flow charts to help with sequencing and developing automaticity of activities
- design simple annotations or story-boards to show sequences in an activity
- provide blank copies of diagrams, charts etc. for completion, clearly indicating where information should go
- provide personal checklists for equipment required – link with timetable to devise a 'daily' bag packing list
- use a flowchart to show a systematic approach to observation/data processing
- allow dyslexic students to verbalise as they carry out practical activities – even record their comments to help with report writing
- build-in diversions/rest periods to lesson plans to minimise fatigue

FIELD-WORK/INVESTIGATION

Barriers to learning: some dyslexic students may
- be unable to remember timetables, rules and instructions for carrying out e.g. classroom investigations/fieldwork
- have difficulty organising/consulting several sources of information simultaneously
- have difficulties with prioritising listening, observing and writing (especially note-taking) when undertaking an investigation
- struggle to record good quality information unobtrusively during an observation/ investigation e.g. filling in context details
- experience problems verbalising experience from investigation/observation/ fieldwork notes which may be incomplete and/or illegible

Reasonable Adjustments: teachers might
- talk over the 'rules' for an investigation activity and relate these to a flow chart or numbered checklist following the required sequence of actions
- issue pre-field trip/investigation reading and preparation materials well in advance – including checklists of required equipment
- repeat pronunciation of e.g. place names and field trip specific terms - provide word lists and glossaries of these
- provide a digital recorder for recording observations and comments
- ensure that safety issues are fully understood e.g. rehearse following emergency procedures; arrange first-aid input prior to fieldwork

DIRECTIONALITY AND TIME

Dyslexic difficulties linked to orientation and direction may affect the understanding of patterns, sequences, time and co-ordinates. Dyslexic students may also have difficulty with the vocabulary of directionality, time and sequence.

Barriers to learning: some dyslexic students may
- reverse letters and numbers when writing
- have little or no sense of direction e.g. confusion of left and right
- be unable to cope with spoken or written directions – e.g.' left/right, forward/back etc. – so may be unable to move as directed or direct others effectively
- confuse place/directional terminology – e.g. above/below; forward/back
- have problems reading figures in the correct direction or order
- have difficulty counting backwards
- be unable to sequence the steps in an activity correctly
- become muddled when working on a set task and start over again – more than once
- experience difficulty in learning to use analogue clock or watch
- be unable to judge the passing of time or estimate how long an activity will take

Reasonable adjustments: teachers might
- help students to develop their own strategies for knowing left/right – e.g. **R**ing on **R**ight hand etc.
- use arrows and movement to help with directions
- use visual and kinaesthetic activities like drawing arrows to illustrate the directionality of place/directional words
- issue flow charts/numbered steps for set activities and encourage students to tick each step completed
- use digital clocks initially but introduce comparisons with 'round' clocks
- teach language of time specifically – relate round clock to familiar items like pizza and relate quarter and half hours to sharing
- continually remind students how much time has passed
- use a stopwatch or countdown digital clock to show time actually passing

GROSS/FINE MOTOR SKILLS AND CO-ORDINATION

(Handwriting and graphic skills issues are identified in a separate section below)

Barriers to Learning: dyslexic students may
- experience problems with automaticity in motor skills resulting in clumsiness when moving around and manipulating tools/equipment
- have poor sitting posture, making writing physically difficult
- be unable to do up buttons and tie shoelaces quickly and neatly
- may be unable to co-ordinate or plan fine or gross sequential movements
- be clumsy, bump into things or knock them over when moving around the room

- have great difficulty learning to swim or ride a bike
- struggle with team and ball games – often missing the ball
- have no idea of proportion or scale – affecting drawing accuracy
- have poor depth perception and be unable to judge distance especially in corridors and staircases
- have difficulty estimating speed of moving people/objects on the playing field or in traffic
- experience weaknesses and increasing fatigue over the course of the day

Reasonable adjustments:
- use multi-sensory teaching strategies whenever possible
- remain aware of the implications of students' fine/gross motor problems when planning classroom activities
- create wide aisles in the classroom to prevent mishaps
- allow dyslexic students extra desk space to help with organisation of work
- build-in mini-breaks, diversions/rest periods to minimise fatigue - encourage students to put pencils down and shake out their hands
- arrange additional hands-on time for dyslexic students to practice skills and techniques so they may become proficient in the use of equipment
- provide templates to develop kinaesthetic familiarity with shapes etc.
- demonstrate and model techniques often e.g. to show a tennis stroke
- break down tasks/movements into a series of very small steps and model these
- help learners develop rhythm to develop co-ordination and automaticity in practical activities - e.g. use music, beating time, tapping feet etc. – even develop a dance routine for e.g. setting up a science experiment
- when practical/complex physical activities are planned, give dyslexic students advance notice so they may rehearse the movements involved
- involve peers in developing strategies for inclusion of dyslexic students in team games
- be sensitive to the embarrassment of dyslexic students in some activities e.g. asking them to take off shoes
- introduce strategies to help students determine their own position in space in relation to others
- develop exercises that will help students to anticipate common hazards like doors opening towards them, passing people on stairs etc.
- teach road safety in a multi-sensory way, ensuring that dyslexic students use all their senses to decide when it is safe to cross a road

Note: Teachers' use of multi-sensory teaching methods will enable dyslexic students to use their strengths to support difficulties in other areas – for example, a student with weak visual processing may compensate for this with strong auditory verbal skills.

HANDWRITING

Many students with dyslexia find the mechanical aspects of writing a problem. Graphic skills are poor and writing is slow, laboured and non-automatic, lacking fluency. There are some students for whom handwriting is a physical and emotional struggle. Not only may handwriting be illegible, but words and letter strings may be transposed. Diagrams may be wrongly proportioned or reversed and columns may be misaligned. Dyslexic students may produce unusual spatial organisation of the page with words widely spaced or tightly pushed together, margins are often ignored and writing is not on the line.

Barriers to written performance: when writing, dyslexic students may
- have illegible handwriting and poor layout of written work
- have neat handwriting, but write very slowly
- have difficulty forming letters
- have an awkward pencil grip – resulting in weakness, pain and fatigue in hand/wrist and deteriorating legibility when writing at length
- have an unusual pencil grip, e.g. the thumb on top of the fingers (a "fist grip") and grip the pencil so tightly that the hand cramps
- press so hard when writing that the paper tears
- put their head down on the desk to watch the tip of the pencil as they write
- write letters with unusual starting and ending points
- have great difficulty getting letters to "sit" on the horizontal lines
- confuse upper and lower case letters and have difficulty remembering how to form capital cursive letters
- tightly pack writing into one area of the page instead of being evenly spread out
- telescope letters, perhaps omitting vowels
- be unable to write continuously without frequent rests
- take an unusually long time to write anything
- transpose words and letter strings

Reasonable adjustments: teachers might
- issue offer a range of cushioned/shaped pencil grips or special pens for writing
- give lots of practice writing individual letters/numbers which are often reversed
- encourage students to put pencils down and shake out their hands
- issue blank jotters and paper **only** if students request them
- provide blank copies of diagrams, charts etc. for completion, clearly indicating where responses should go
- accept alternatives to hand-written responses e.g. a mind map, recorded response or a drawing/diagram
- ensure that dyslexic students have access to ICT for all writing activities
- do not penalise a dyslexic student for poor presentation of work or bizarre spelling

Note: Subject teachers are not expected to teach dyslexic students handwriting but, where graphic skills are part of the subject curriculum, they may teach strategies for improving this.

SELF-ESTEEM ISSUES

For many learners with dyslexia the experience of success in the classroom may be rare. Self-esteem and confidence issues and the cumulative effect of fatigue may have a powerful impact on dyslexic students' ability to cope with some of the demands of the secondary curriculum. Students with dyslexia often consider themselves to be failures and the stress they endure in the classroom impacts on their motivation, emotional well-being and their behavioural stability. Many are working constantly at the limits of their endurance and may rarely - or never - experience success in the classroom.

Barriers to learning: dyslexic students may
- expect to fail at set tasks, so are reluctant to try anything new
- lack stamina and be vulnerable to fatigue
- lack self-confidence and have a poor self-image
- experience stress that results in reading/writing/oral skills to deteriorate
- be disappointed at a poor return for their efforts
- be embarrassed and feel humiliated if their difficulties are exposed in class

Learners with dyslexia may experience despair and exhaustion and be unable to keep up the level of alertness and forward planning needed to sustain intricate coping strategies. When coping strategies fail, dyslexia may be expressed by inappropriate diversionary behaviour.

Reasonable adjustments: teachers might
- remain aware of students' learning profiles and of the nature of individual strengths as well as dyslexic issues
- offer encouragement and support for all activities
- encourage and praise oral contributions - praise effort as well as work well done
- mark on **content** not presentation of work
- **never** ask students with dyslexia to undertake tasks that might expose them to public failure and humiliation e.g. reading aloud without adequate prep time

It is important that subject teachers remain alert for difficult situations and defuse any possibly embarrassing circumstances that could result in aggressive or withdrawn behaviour.

FURTHER READING

Beech, J (2013) *The Little Book of Dyslexia: Both sides of the classroom* Edited by Ian Gilbert. Independent Thinking Press, Crown House Publishing
Joe Beech was diagnosed with both dyslexia and dyspraxia at age seven and is now a physics teacher. This book is full of practical ideas that can be used by teachers in the classroom.

MacKay, N (2005) *Removing Dyslexia as a Barrier to Achievement: The Dyslexia Friendly Schools Toolkit* 3rd Edition (2012) Wakefield, SEN Marketing

Pavey, B (2012) *The Dyslexia-Friendly Teacher's Toolkit* London, Sage
This book is a really practical, hands-on guide packed with a wealth of advice on strategies and "things to try" reflecting the author's extensive experience.

Peer, L & Reid, G (2000) *Multilingualism, Literacy and Dyslexia: A Challenge for Educators* London, David Fulton Publishers
This work offers advice on approaches and support strategies for dyslexic and bilingual learners learning English as an additional language.

Reid, G (2013) *Dyslexia and Inclusion Classroom approaches for assessment, teaching and learning* (2nd Edition) Abingdon, Routledge
Now fully updated, this book aims to equip all teachers with the necessary knowledge of dyslexia in order to for it to be effectively understood and dealt with in the classroom.

Reid, G & Green, S (2007) 100 Ideas *for Supporting Pupils with Dyslexia* London, Continuum

Rooke, M (2015) *Creative Successful Dyslexic* London, Jessica Kingsley Publishers
Well-known people talk about how dyslexia affected their childhoods and how they overcame the challenges and used the special strengths of dyslexia to achieve great success in adulthood.

Thomson, M (2007) *Supporting Students with Dyslexia at Secondary School – every class teacher's guide to removing barriers and raising attainment* London, Routledge Ch. 5 & 6

Thomson, M (2008) *Dyslexia and Inclusion at Secondary School* IN Reid et al (Ed) 2008 *The SAGE Handbook of Dyslexia* London, Sage

West, T G (1997) *In the Mind's Eye: Visual Thinkers, Gifted People with Learning Difficulties, Computer Images and the Ironies of Creativity* Loughton, Prometheus

DYSLEXIA INDICATORS AT THE SECONDARY STAGE (PHOTOCOPIABLE)

Dyslexia is more than an isolated defect in reading or spelling. The problem may be perceptual, auditory receptive, memory-based or a processing deficit.

Subject teachers are not expected to be able to diagnose these difficulties as such, but some general indications are listed below. If several of these are observed frequently in the classroom, subject teachers should tick the relevant boxes to identify issues when referring a student for further investigation.

Student Name: _____ Class: _____ Date: _____

- ❑ Quality of written work does not adequately reflect the known ability of the student in the subject

- ❑ Good orally but very little written work is produced – many incomplete assignments

- ❑ Disappointing performance in timed tests and other assessments

- ❑ Poor presentation of work – e.g. illegibility, mixed upper and lower case, unequal spacing, copying errors, misaligned columns (especially in Maths)

- ❑ Poor organisational skills – the student is unable to organise self or work efficiently; carries either all books or wrong ones; frequently forgets to hand in work

- ❑ Sequencing poor – student appears to jump from one theme to another, apparently for no reason

- ❑ Inability to memorise (especially in Maths and Modern Languages) even after repeated practice

- ❑ Inability to hold numbers in short-term memory while performing calculations

- ❑ Symbol and shape confusion (especially in Maths)

- ❑ Complains of headaches when reading; sometimes sees patterns/distortions in printed text; says that words move around the page or that text is glaring at them

- ❑ Unable to carry out operations one day which were previously done adequately

- ❑ Unable to take in and carry out more than one instruction at a time

- ❑ Poor depth perception – e.g. clumsy and uncoordinated, bumps into things, difficulty judging distance, catching balls, etc.

- ❑ Poor self-image – lacking in confidence, fear of new situations – may erase large quantities of written work, which is acceptable to the teacher

❑ Tires quickly and work seems to be a disproportionate return for the effort involved in producing it

❑ Easily distracted – either hyperactive or daydreaming

❑ **Other – details below**

Teacher: _____ Subject: _____

Action/information requested:

❑ details of known SEND and support required

❑ investigation of SEND and advice on graduated support

❑ dyslexia assessment

❑ profile of learning needs

❑ suggest reasonable adjustments to be made in class

❑ suggest learning objectives and outcomes for SEN plan

❑ advice re Access arrangements